The Best Clown in Town

By Tom Bradley
Illustrated by Vanessa Lubach

🜊 Dominie Press, Inc.

Publisher: Raymond Yuen
Editor: Bob Rowland
Designer: Mark Deutman
Illustrator: Vanessa Lubach
Cover Designer: Carol Anne Craft

Copyright ©1999 Dominie Press, Inc. All rights reserved. No part of this publication may be reproduced or transmitted in any form or by any means without permission in writing from the publisher. Reproduction of any part of this book, through photocopy, recording, or any electronic or mechanical retrieval system, without the written permission of the publisher, is an infringement of the copyright law.

Published by:

Dominie Press, Inc.

1949 Kellogg Avenue
Carlsbad, California 92008 USA

ISBN 0-7685-0315-9

Printed in Singapore by PH Productions Pte Ltd

2 3 4 5 6 IP 01

TABLE OF CONTENTS

Chapter One
The Chance of a Lifetime   4

Chapter Two
A Trip to the Costume Shop   6

Chapter Three
An Outfit Fit for a Clown   12

Chapter Four
What Else Could Go Wrong?   19

Chapter Five
Keep Smiling   30

Chapter Six
Sally's Soggy Performance   37

Chapter Seven
And the Winner Is   45

Chapter One
The Chance of a Lifetime

Sally Marvin's eyes lit up as she read the poster:

'THE BEST CLOWN IN TOWN'
CONTEST
THIS SATURDAY
SPECIAL JUDGE, ROKKO THE CLOWN
SCHOOL GYM, 2 P.M.

Sally loved clowns, and Rokko was her favorite. She'd seen him many times at the circus. Sally dreamed of being a clown one day. She'd never been onstage or performed in front of an audience, but she was sure that one day she would be able to do it.

Now, it seemed, that day had arrived.

Sally decided that *she* would be the Best Clown in Town! All she needed was the best costume, the best makeup, and the best props.

And the biggest smile.

Chapter Two

A Trip to the Costume Shop

Sally wanted to go to the costume rental shop right after school, but the family car was being repaired that day. It wasn't until the next afternoon that Sally and her Mom were able to go to the shop.

When they arrived, Sally felt as though she had wandered into a magic kingdom. There were hundreds of costumes inside. She could be anything she wanted to be–a pirate, an astronaut, a skeleton, even a cat.

"I want to be a clown," Sally told the clerk.

"The Best Clown in Town?" the man asked, for he knew about the contest.

Sally grinned and nodded her head.

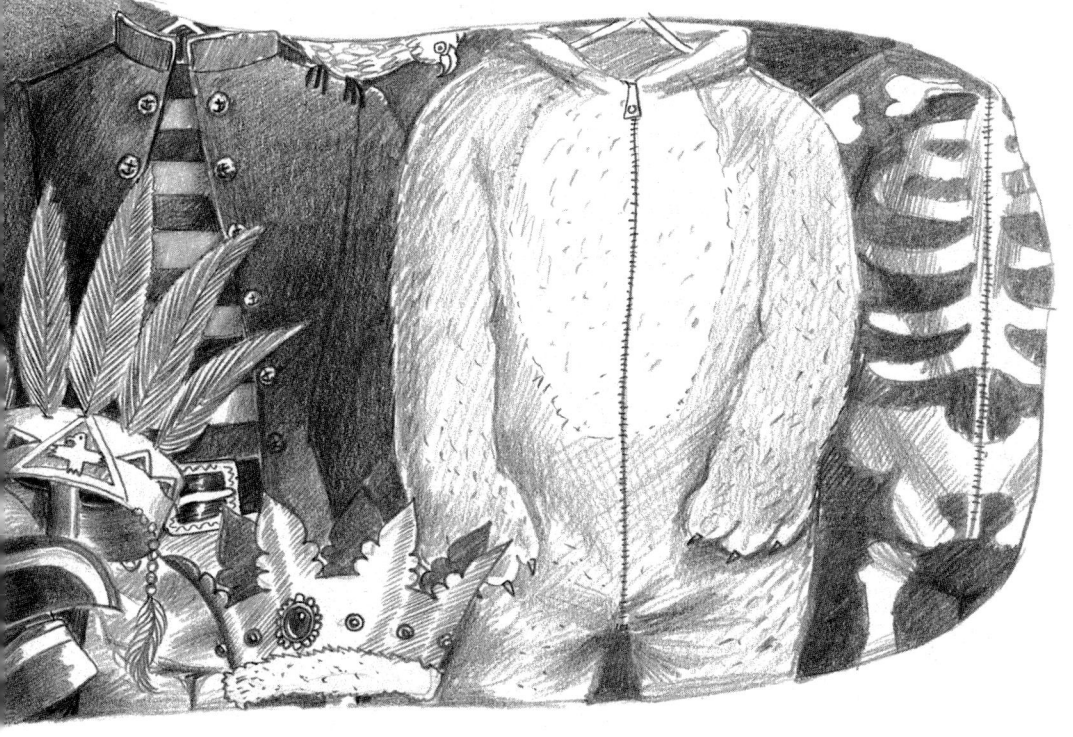

Then the man pulled out a book with pictures of the two basic clown styles that were available.

Sally had a choice. She could be a cheerful, colorful clown with baggy clothes and bright makeup. Or she could be a quiet, pale clown with white makeup, a pointy hat, and a ruffle around her neck.

"Do you have more clown costumes to choose from?" Sally asked.

"The best selection in town," the man said. "We keep them in a special Clown Room. Follow me."

Sally and her Mom followed the clerk into the special Clown Room. But as they walked in, the man suddenly stopped. The room was almost empty!

"Sorry," the clerk said, looking embarrassed. "I wasn't here yesterday. It seems we had a big run on clown costumes. What you see here is all we've got left."

Sally wanted to cry. Because of the problems with the car, she'd arrived too late to get the best clown costume. Without the best costume, how could she win the contest?

She looked at the bits and pieces left behind, unwanted by the other would-be Best Clowns in Town. There wasn't much to choose from: a pair of oversized shoes with worn-out soles, and a bright red wig with large empty patches where the hair had fallen out.

"Maybe we can rent these and make the rest of the costume ourselves," Mom said.

Sally sighed. "The contest is for the Best Clown in Town, Mom. Not the *worst*."

Just then, Sally heard someone in the next room asking about a clown costume. She had to make up her mind in a hurry. If she didn't take what was left, the next person would.

"OK," she said. "We'll take them."

Chapter Three
An Outfit Fit for a Clown

During the next few days, Sally spent every spare moment putting together her clown costume. She found an old pair of her father's plaid golf pants and shortened the legs with a pair of scissors.

The pants were bright and baggy. "Perfect!" Sally said, smiling. She borrowed a pair of her father's bright orange suspenders to hold up the loose-fitting pants.

She and Mom went to a yard sale, where she bought a big suit jacket and an old hat with a turned-up brim. When they got home, she sewed colored patches onto the jacket to brighten it up.

Then she sewed the red wig to the inside of the hat so that the hair would hang down around her face. She found her old paint set and decorated the hat with brightly colored stripes.

She glued oversized soles onto the rented shoes. Sally smiled as she climbed into her costume.

"Keep working on the smile," she told herself. "Clowns smile a *lot*." When she put on her clown makeup, her smile was even bigger. She put white powder all over her face, and then painted on a big red smile. Finally, she drew huge eyebrows above her eyes, and tied on the red nose she had made from a painted ball.

When she thought everything looked just right, she took off her costume and hung it up. Then she spent the rest of the day practicing her clown tricks. Sally already knew how to juggle. For the contest, she would juggle three oranges.

She found a bucket and cut up sheets of paper to make confetti. The confetti-in-the-bucket trick was a favorite among clowns. She'd pretend that the bucket was filled with water and threaten to throw it over the audience. They would duck and scream, but the only thing to come pouring out of the bucket would be a shower of confetti.

Sally could already imagine herself onstage for the first time in her life. She imagined the audience roaring with laughter. She could see Rokko handing her the prize for being the Best Clown in Town.

All she had to do was wait one more day.

Chapter Four

What Else Could Go Wrong?

On Saturday, the day of the contest, it rained.

Sally needed a big umbrella to stay dry as she ran from the house to the car in full clown makeup and costume.

She had two oranges in her baggy pants pockets and one in her oversized jacket. In another jacket pocket, she had stuffed the paper bag filled with confetti.

She decided that she would put the confetti in the bucket just before she stepped onto the stage. That way, it wouldn't blow away or get wet.

Sally jumped into the car and threw the empty bucket onto the back seat.

"Let's go," she said, as Mom got into the car.

"Cross your fingers and hope that it gets us there," said Mom.

The school gym was about five minutes away by car. When they were halfway there, the engine started sputtering.

"Oh, no," said Mom. As they turned a corner, the car died completely and Mom had to steer it off to the side of the road.

"Sorry, Sally," said Mom. "By the time we get help, it will be too late for the contest."

But Sally wasn't ready to give up so easily–not after all the trouble she'd gone to.

"I can make it on my own from here," she said. "It's only a few more blocks."

"OK," said Mom. "But be careful."

Sally grabbed the umbrella and her bucket from the back seat and opened the car door. She could still make it to the contest on time.

If she hurried.

As Sally turned the first corner, a gust of wind pulled at the umbrella, making it hard to hold on to. Especially since she needed one hand to carry the bucket.

She kept moving, all the while trying to keep her costume dry.

Around the next corner, she passed a very large dog–a dog the size of a small horse! The dog barked twice and started to chase her, snapping at her oversized heels.

Sally glanced over her shoulder and yelled in fright. She didn't see the crack in the sidewalk.

She tripped and fell on her face when one of her clown shoes got caught in the crack. She managed to hang on to the bucket, but the umbrella slipped out of her hand and blew inside out. It was ruined!

Sally jumped to her feet and faced the big dog, which had stopped just a few feet away.

Sally shivered. The dog looked big enough to eat her, she thought.

Eat! Suddenly, she remembered the oranges.

Sally pulled an orange from her jacket pocket and threw it as hard as she could over the dog's head. And the dog, thinking that this was a game, spun around and raced off to catch the orange.

Sally left the umbrella on the sidewalk, grabbed the bucket, and ran.

Without the umbrella to protect her, Sally could feel the rain soaking through her hat, her jacket, and her baggy pants. And the rain was seeping through her shoes. One of the soles had come loose when she fell.

The rain was coming down heavier, but Sally didn't stop. She *couldn't* stop. She was almost at the school gym. She couldn't turn back now. "After all," she told herself, "the worst of it is over."

What else could possibly go wrong?

Chapter Five

Keep Smiling

Sally ran the last hundred yards to the gym and dashed into the hallway. She couldn't believe her eyes. Dozens of would-be clowns were there. Many of them wore costumes from the rental shop Sally had visited. Some of the little clowns wore brightly colored makeup like Sally's. Others wore white powder on their faces.

To Sally, every one of them seemed better dressed than she was. And their smiles were dazzling.

"They can afford to smile," thought Sally. "They don't look like drowned rats."

Before anyone noticed she was there, Sally ran off to the bathroom to check the damage to her costume. What she saw in the mirror made her heart sink.

The painted stripes on her hat had run together, and the upturned brim was soggy and sagging. It looked as though she'd shoved an old bowl onto her head.

The ends of the wig underneath the hat hung down in loose, wet strands like drowned rats' tails.

Most of Sally's makeup was still in place. So was her red nose. But the water had ruined the lining of her jacket. Now it was baggy and lumpy. And she already knew about the damage done to her shoes.

Sally wanted to run out of the bathroom, past the other clowns, and keep running until she got home. But then she thought of Rokko the Clown, the contest judge. He was her favorite clown. Would he give up so easily?

Sally decided to wait and see what the other contestants did for their acts onstage. "I might not look as good as the rest of the clowns, but maybe I can outperform them," she thought.

"Keep smiling," she said to herself. "You've got to keep smiling."

Since she was the last clown to arrive, Sally would be the last to perform. She stood at the back of the gym, watching the other contestants go through their paces.

Some of the clowns were mimes who walked through invisible doorways. Others pretended to tiptoe along invisible tightropes or pick up heavy weights.

Some pulled enormous long handkerchiefs out of bottomless pockets. One played the accordion. One beat a drum. Another played a trumpet. None of the other clowns juggled. And no one else did the confetti trick.

Sally saw her Mom arrive just as it was her turn to go onstage. Suddenly, she remembered the bag of confetti in her jacket pocket. As she pulled out the paper bag, she *should* have noticed that it had gotten soaked in the rain, like everything else. And she *should* have noticed that the confetti was wet when she dumped it into the bucket.

But Sally was in too much of a hurry to notice much, except that her name had just been called.

Bucket in hand, she headed for the stage.

Chapter Six

Sally's Soggy Performance

When Sally ran onto the stage and faced the audience, she heard people starting to laugh. Even Rokko, dressed in his own clown costume, was laughing.

That's when Sally froze. It started in her toes and slowly worked its way up her body. Her first time onstage, and she had stage fright. Sally was petrified!

Sally waved her arms in the air, signaling to the audience that she was about to juggle. Her arms felt stiff and heavy. She thought she must look like a puppet on a string.

She forced one hand into her baggy pants to grab an orange. But as she pulled out the first orange, she felt the juice running through her fingers. It had been smashed when she fell.

The audience laughed.

"Smile!" Sally told herself as she pulled out the second orange. It was more mashed than the first one.

She looked at the two lumps of orange pulp in her hands. How could she juggle mashed oranges? She tried to toss them into the air, but they plopped right back into her palms.

The audience kept laughing.

Sally wanted to cry. She shook her head, trying to make everyone stop laughing. Couldn't they see that this was no laughing matter?!

But they laughed even louder.

This clown contest had turned into a disaster!

All Sally wanted to do was finish her act and rush off the stage. She forced herself to grab the bucket and pretend that it was full of water.

Then she started to stomp around the stage. But it was hard to stomp with the sole of one shoe flopping along with every step.

Sally ignored the shoe and pretended that she was about to dump a bucket of water on the people in the front row.

Some of the children squealed and tried to duck for cover. As Sally stomped to the center of the stage, the sole of her shoe finally came loose. It took off like a floppy missile and was headed straight for Rokko's head! The clown judge ducked as the sole flew over his head and landed in the lap of the woman sitting behind him.

The audience screamed with laughter.

Sally felt sick. She just wanted to empty the bucket of confetti and run off the stage. Now! She closed her eyes and flung the bucket to send the confetti flying over the audience. She heard a little squeal, and then silence.

Sally opened her eyes and looked in the bucket. The confetti was still there. She looked out at the sea of faces looking back at her. The audience was wondering what was going on. And so was Sally!

This was the final embarrassment, she thought. First the oranges, and now this.

With a shout of frustration, Sally drew back and flung the bucket–this time with all her might.

And this time, the confetti *did* come out.

In a solid, wet blob.

Straight into Rokko's face. He was so surprised, he didn't have time to duck.

Sally screamed and ran for her life.

Chapter Seven

And the Winner Is ....

Half an hour later, after Rokko had cleaned himself up, he stood onstage with the contestants to award the prize for the Best Clown in Town. Sally stayed near the back of the stage, where she couldn't be easily seen. This had been the most embarrassing day of her life!

Rokko spoke to the audience, explaining how he had judged one of the contestants as the best clown.

"Some of these clowns have the best costumes I've ever seen," said Rokko, looking around. "And big smiles to match."

The audience cheered.

"But the best clowns don't always wear the fanciest costumes or have the biggest smiles," Rokko said.

"Sometimes clowns are sad, especially when things go wrong. But no matter how bad things are, they keep trying. And that makes a great clown."

He paused. "Like our winner today. The Best Clown in Town. Sally Marvin!"

Rokko grabbed Sally's hand and pulled her forward to take a bow.

But just then, Sally tripped and took Rokko down with her in a heap.

And to her surprise, that brought the biggest laugh of all!